The Angelic Interface

by

Stella Zingas

Published by BeeleeveBooks
Copyright © 2016 Stella Zingas
All rights reserved.
ISBN: 978-0-9956420-2-7

The Angelic Interface

Introduction

The use of the word 'interface', which literally means 'between sides', has been used here to denote the forming of a link between the ethereal or invisible realm and our own earthly life.

This first collection of anecdotes follows the theme of how the angelic realm interacts with us, not only to assist in the more crucial decisions of events we encounter, but also in the more mundane, everyday problems that, unknown to us, may have important repercussions in the future that we cannot know of yet.

Each story here is exactly as it happened and nothing has been embellished or exaggerated in any way.

If you have ever had the thought 'Now what were the chances of THAT ever happening!' after something extraordinary had taken place, you might like to reconsider that it may not have been mere coincidence or unbelievably good luck but that it could have been angelic intervention coming to your aid as you tried to steer a path through those difficult obstacles in your life.

My motive for publishing these personal experiences is to make it better known that we can all benefit from the awareness of how events in our lives can be influenced by the higher echelons of the spirit world and how we can be comforted by the knowledge that help is at hand, no matter how mundane the problem may appear.

It strikes me that the more we ask for help from this source, the more we may receive, whether from our own guardian angel or from one of the 'big guns' such as Archangel Michael. Our loved ones in spirit also have their role to play, whether we know of them or not. In addition to these dear souls there is a multitude of discarnate beings who may also wish to be of loving service to us, perhaps within the remit of their earthly professions, eg. a doctor, teacher, priest, etc; or even to fulfil some karmic debt as part of a higher plan concerning their own spiritual development.

My understanding of this angelic assistance is that it is part and parcel of what I sometimes think of as "the God system", and is known by many names - the Holy Spirit, Christ Consciousness, Life Force, and so on. For me it is of one and the same essence. All we have to do is tap into this bottomless well with a sincere heart, a pure motive and a willingness to put our own personal effort into the mix and our ego to one side.

I hope that some of you will come to realise that rather than calling such an occurrence 'an amazing coincidence' or 'fate', that whatever has happened is an act of love from the Source-of-All-That-Is via the angelic hierarchy, providing the most extraordinary synchronicities that defy explanation. Perhaps it will make you more aware of the truth as stated in the scriptures - "Ask, and it shall be given unto you", but remember that the answers will always be for the higher good than for personal gain or selfish motives.

You may well have your own examples of this benevolent intervention at work in your life. The following stories are simply some of my own personal experiences and it is my hope that you will be able to identify with some of them and draw parallels with your own personal life events.

The Angelic Interface

Chapter 1

Who is your guardian angel?

It is interesting that the ancient Greek word for 'messenger' is 'angelos', the word from which 'angel' is derived. So when people talk of receiving messages from their angels, they are not wrong; except that, unfortunately, they are often viewed as entities in themselves rather than emissaries from the Godhead and part of what was called 'the heavenly host'. I find it such a pity that today's attitude is to isolate these beings as individual entities unattached to any higher (I should say 'highest') spiritual figurehead or overall governing body.

We should do well to remember that one third of the angelic kingdom chose to leave with Lucifer at the time of his expulsion. Anyone who has studied Latin will know that 'Lucifer' is a direct translation of 'Light-bearer' (lux/lucis meaning light/of the light, and ferer the verb to bear), but he was renamed Satan as he had chosen to no longer be a bearer of light but instead to wreak havoc with humanity as his revenge; and some would say he is doing an excellent job of that when we look at our daily world events. So my advice when getting in touch with your angel is to make sure they are from the right source by involving Christ's/God's Holy name in your opening prayer. Sadly, much negative work has been carried out by these fallen ones as they delight in influencing gullible or naive people by impersonating higher angelic beings. Their role is to mislead humankind, to wrong-foot us in our decisions, ambitions and goals. I have even known them to impersonate well-known spiritual guides (the likes of Silver Birch, White Eagle, etc) and thus mislead and misinform the spiritually vulnerable. By this, I mean those persons who might be desperate for guidance and who will cling to the first thing that appears to want to help them, but sadly, only leading them into a prolonged misery.

No wonder the scriptures instruct us not to be engaged with 'spirits', because it is extremely difficult to be certain of what you are dealing with. It is for this reason that I have become very wary of any channeling that takes place outside the protection of God's will and the love of the Christ.

If you are in any doubt, then please use the Lord's Prayer (and say it with full conviction and meaning) when you open up to any angelic guidance. You could also use the colour gold to surround yourself as it carries the highest degree of protection. Guard against any guidance that simply boosts your ego or suggests you trample over others to get what you want. This obviously comes from the wrong source but sometimes we become blind to this truth when we only seek selfish gain. Take great care my friends, and remember it is "THY will be done..." not MY will be done.

Chapter 2

Saved by a coin

Many years ago, back in the mid 1970s, I went to visit friends, who were living in Andorra, for the New Year. One of the chaps was a ski instructor so we all went to spend the day on the slopes. His particular resort could only be reached by a mountain ski lift. It was an automated system and coin-operated, and was a great way to be transported from the road up to the resort and take in the wonderful view at the same time.

I had never been on a pair of skis in my life and decided that this was **not** the time to start, so I decided instead to hire a toboggan and have my own fun. There was a long row of bright orange molded plastic toboggans for hire and right at the end was a scruffy old wooden one with a bit of rope for a handle. That was the one for me and off I plodded to find an area well away from the ski piste.

Every time I hit a hidden boulder, I fell off and found myself thigh deep in snow which was tricky to climb out of. Giggling away to myself, I scrambled after my sledge which had scooted away ahead of me, and this happened several times. I was so carried away that I did not realise that I had lost my bearings and could no longer see another soul nor the piste. There were more pine trees dotted about and the ground had become much steeper. Having hit a tree root, I fell off again but this time my sledge sped away on its own down through the sloping wood. I intrepidly climbed down after it but when I reached it, I realised I would not be able to retrace my steps back up to the top as it was too difficult to climb while holding on to this heavy wooden toboggan. There was only one thing for it to keep on going down through the pine forest.

Eventually, I could see flatter farm land below but I had to cross a stream first. I walked along it for quite a way before there was a place shallow enough and with boulders where I could cross. I then trekked across two fields to the road but there wasn't a car in sight to hitch a lift. In the distance, about 2 or 3 kilometres away, I could make out the ski lift so I set off dragging my sledge with me. When I finally reached the roadside ski lift station, I remembered to my horror, that it needed a coin! There was not a soul in sight and by now, some two hours later, I knew my friends would be worried and looking for me at the top so there was no point waiting for them down at the roadside. And, of course, there was no such thing as a mobile phone in those days. I was well and truly stranded. I also had no bag or purse with me, but in a frantic search, I checked all my pockets. To my utter amazement and relief, in a pocket in my jeans, I found ONE coin and it was, by some miracle, the **exact coin** needed to operate the ski lift barrier. Now what were the chances of THAT happening?

I went up the side of the mountain for the second time that day, still clutching the old wooden sledge which was not easy while dangling in a ski lift chair! At the top, I soon espied my three friends standing in a line and all gravely staring into the distance looking for me.

I quietly joined in at the end of the line until they noticed me and after much consternation on their part, followed by laughter when I told them of my adventure, we all headed off to the bar for a round of warming Spanish brandy at 45p per shot. (Mind you, you could buy a whole bottle of it in any supermarket for the same price!).

I didn't know much about guardian angels in those days, except that I had been told of many spiritual guides and helpers who came in and out of my life as circumstances dictated. I am absolutely certain that one of them was looking after me that day. So many things could have gone horribly wrong throughout that escapade as it was fraught with potential danger at every turn, but it was 'all's well that ends well', and 40 years on I still remember it like it was only last winter, as one of those extremely lucky saves in my life.

Chapter 3

In Andalucia

Back in the early 1990s, I found myself facing another Christmas alone so instead, I took a flight to Malaga with a rough idea of where I wanted to visit in Andalucia. What transpired were some interesting occurrences involving the invisible world of spirit that makes the telling of this trip more than just a travel story. I began by taking a Greyhound bus to the mountain town of Ronda and spent a wonderful three days exploring this historic and stunningly beautiful place perched high above the river valley below. No-one spoke English and I had to manage with my Spanish phrase book and some French but I got by. At the train station, the ticket man was trying to explain to me with difficulty that going to Granada involved a change at Antiquera and that there was a possibility that the trains would not connect and I could be stranded there. I decided to risk it, though after a half hour of watching imaginary tumbleweed blowing along the deserted platform in the middle of nowhere it became somewhat worrying. But, mercifully, I was in luck.

After finding a rather seedy little hotel in the middle of Granada, I set off to explore the magnificent Alhambra, a jaw-dropping Moorish citadel full of exquisite buildings, sculptures of wood and stone carvings, fountains and gardens, including the intricate art-work all dedicated to the name of Allah. My admission ticket was valid for two days as there was so much to see. As

I sat in the beautiful Summer Palace gardens with their yew tree walks, canals and fountains, and the local stray cats who were helping me to eat my ham baguette, I felt a tremor. I mused absent-mindedly that I hadn't realised Granada had a Metro subway. Then I snapped into the reality that, of course it didn't; it was in fact a small earthquake!

During the night, I'd had two experiences that were more than just dreams. One was of a German Shepherd dog that suddenly and very ferociously barked and it woke me up with a start. The second experience was of seeing a young man wearing a light blue denim jacket who was standing with his back to me. I asked him who he was and he turned around, smiled and said "Carlos". Then he was gone.

Back at the Alhambra for the second day, I visited the Alcazar, the fortress, and a custodian followed me around nervously. He then beckoned me to visit the dungeon and as I stood inside he closed the door, locked it and then held up the massive iron key with a creepy, sinister look on his face. I feel certain, in hindsight, that had I shown any fear or terror, he would have derived some kind of perverse pleasure from it; but instead, I fixed him with a look that silently said "Really?" and he let me out with a sheepish look on his face. I don't believe I was in any danger but he had definitely overstepped his line of duty. Later that same day, I looked across the grounds and saw him being led away, firmly held either side by either fellow custodians or police (the uniform looked similar), and he looked the worse for alcohol and was in a tearful state. My guess is he tried his little trick (or worse) with some other woman and they had reported him. What a poor tortured soul, but I wonder if this was what the German Shepherd dog was guarding me against. However, when I returned home to the UK I found out that my friend who had a rescued dog of the same breed, had had to have him put down because he had bitten someone, pretty much the exact same time as when I saw him in the 'dream'. Perhaps what I experienced was linked to this in some way. I'd had a fondness for this dog as he was so kind and patient with a kitten who used to play with his tail. I firmly believe that there is no such thing as a vicious dog, only a vicious owner. The poor thing was only doing what he had been previously taught to do, before being rescued. Shame on those people.

On my way home from the Alhambra, I went into a bar for a refreshing mint tea. It was empty except for three local lads who were busy talking and laughing. I had been pondering how much I would have liked to visit the Arab quarters of the Albecin but had been warned that, back then, it was not a safe place for a woman on her own and I had also accepted that going to the gypsy caves to watch Flamenco was even more taboo as previous tourists had been robbed at knife-point. Eventually, one of the guys started to talk to me and although he did not speak English and I did not speak Spanish, we managed a simple conversation in French. He offered to take me that evening to the Albecin and my intuition felt that it was fine to accept. We agreed to meet later and as I left the bar, something made me turn back to look at it and I saw that the bar was called

'Cafe Carlos', the same name as my ethereal visitor and I felt so sure that I was being guided and being kept safe. And indeed, I was safe with this young chap who escorted me through the quaint winding streets. We drank tea in one of the Arab tea houses where we were seated amongst a festoon of oriental rugs, vibrant wall-hangings and colourful antique lamps. We rounded the evening off with a visit to a lively bar and he was good company and a perfect gentleman seeing me back to my hotel.

By Christmas Eve I had travelled down to the coastal town of Almunecar where there were a few more tourists about and I could be sure of restaurants staying open over the Christmas period. On Christmas Day during an outdoor lunch, I met an elderly lady from Estonia and although she had never been to England, she spoke perfect English (plus several other languages) and looked like a character out of an Agatha Christie novel with her lace collar and mink stole fastened with a jeweled brooch. After chatting with her and her friend, she invited me for lunch at her home in a few days' time, which I happily accepted. I have fond memories of this lady in her 80s leisurely making pancakes using beer, which we ate with avocados and garlic, washed down with a lively local champagne. We talked late into the evening of religious and spiritual matters and we found so much in common and of interest. I stayed in touch with this dear lady for many years and took pleasure in sending her postcards from any special churches or cathedrals that I visited on my subsequent travels.

Back in Almunecar a few days later while walking along the sea front, I heard a van with a loud-speaker and I discovered that it was announcing a Flamenco concert happening that night. I was determined to go as I felt I had missed out in Granada, and as it was to be held in one of the mountain villages a few miles away, I went there by taxi but knowing there would be no taxis coming back. It turned out to be one of the most memorable evenings of my life. There was a small group of performers:- guitarists, a visiting guest male singer who was well-known in Andalucia, and a fabulous female dancer who was superb. The guitarist had long glossy black hair and thick curled eyelashes and looked exactly how you'd expect a true gypsy to look. He was also a stunning musician. The singer had such soul and passion in his voice and the dancer was a whirlwind of flame-red lace as she showed off her skilful footwork. I was absolutely mesmerised by the whole spectacle and it was as if an old smouldering ember in my soul had been rekindled and was now sparkling with sheer joy. What a fabulous evening; however, I had no idea how I was going to get back home. The majority of the audience were Spanish locals, but I espied two fellows who looked like visitors and I boldly asked them where they were headed. with 'luck' again on my side, they were able to give me a lift to within a mile or so of where I was staying so all ended well.

I spent New Year in a town called Nerja, about half way towards Malaga and I witnessed the old Spanish tradition when the clock chimes at midnight. They would eat one grape on the first chime, 2 grapes on the second chime, 4 on the third, 8 on the fourth and so on until their mouths were crammed with munched up grapes that they could not possibly eat and swallow in time to get the next lot all in - a completely impossible task but they still tried! Then a live rock band struck up some real stomping music on a stage in the town square and everyone danced their socks off and drank champagne. It was great fun to watch. A German family next to me offered me a plastic flute of champagne and I was pleased that I remembered how to say "Happy New Year" in German.

To sum up, my advice would be that instead of staying put just because it's Christmas, try branching out on a little adventure. My trip of almost 20 years ago turned out to be one of the most enjoyable in my life. I saw many wonderful things, met lovely people, experienced a slice of history and felt the thrill of seeing live Flamenco at its most authentic. And through it all, I felt that I was being looked after in some ethereal way, and those kind of experiences for me are always priceless.

Chapter 4

Synchronicity

About five years ago, I was in the unenviable position of finding myself very dissatisfied and unhappy with a recent move within Glastonbury and I knew I had to move on yet again. Frantic and extensive property searches were all in vain and I was reaching what is known in the I-Ching as 'the crescendo of awfulness'. One morning, in the process of awakening, I clearly heard these words in my head: "I am the Angel of Help Harinas!". I began a search online to try to find out anything about the name Harinas. To my surprise, the name of a small town in Mexico came up called 'Coatepec Harinas'. As I dug deeper, I read that its original name was 'Coauhtepetl' which meant 'Serpent Hill' in the old language of Nahuantl and I was able to actually see this hill just outside the town, on Google Satellite. I found the connection between this name of Serpent Hill and the fact that Glastonbury Tor is also connected to the myth of the coiled 'worm' or 'serpent' around the Tor absolutely fascinating and evidence of some synchronicity at work. In 1825, the boom of flour production at this town in Mexico caused them to add the word 'Harinas' meaning 'flour' to their town name.

What followed was an extraordinary sequence of events that finally resulted in the sale of my flat despite unforeseeable difficulties at every turn. The closer I came to exchanging contracts on my property, the more difficult things became in trying to find my future accommodation and I knew that it would be impossible to find somewhere in the two weeks between exchange and completion when I would have to leave the premises. The 'crescendo of awfulness' had reached its zenith but help came in the most unexpected and unusual way when I was offered a 'safety net' by an acquaintance who offered to house me and my cat temporarily if the worst came to the worst. This meant a lot to me and was a huge relief. At the eleventh hour, a flat for rent came up in Bruton which I immediately accepted and I viewed my great 'luck' quite literally as a 'God-send'.

There was even one final glitch in that the sale almost fell through at the last minute, even after I had already moved out to the new flat; but again, unseen help was truly at hand. But the story of Harinas, my angelic helper, is not yet ended. Three years later, while on holiday in Skiathos, I discovered that a relationship I had pinned all my hopes upon had crumbled and I was plunged into a very saddened state. I tried to continue with my holiday as best I could and spent a day visiting beautiful little churches and the Monastery of Evangelistra, ending the day with a drink at a cafe in the town with a fellow tourist also on the churches trip. When I got back to my holiday studio, I realised that I had lost one of my earrings at some point during my day out. The next day I went back to the cafe, where I had removed my jumper, in case it had come off in the process, but no luck. It could be anywhere on the island so I gave it up for lost. Two days later I was looking in my cosmetic bag on the dressing table and there it was - the missing earring! There is absolutely no way that it could have dropped in there and it was more than just a surprise to see it. In fact, I was flabberghasted. Later, when I looked in my diary to check my return flight time, I noticed that the following day was the anniversary of when I heard the voice of Harinas four years earlier. Then I had the 'light bulb' moment of making the Mexican connection; I had bought the earrings in Tihuana, Mexico back in the 1970s! So once again, when I was feeling at a very low ebb, I received the clear knowledge that help was being given me. Remember, as I have already mentioned in chapter one, the word 'angel' comes from the Greek 'angelos' meaning messenger and these little messages are to remind us that we are not alone in our sorrows or misfortunes but that we are being helped; even if we cannot 'prove' it to the sometimes cynical attitudes of others. Just know it within yourself, be glad of it and most of all, give thanks.

Chapter 5

The animal kingdom

Most of us know that St Francis of Assisi was linked to the animal kingdom and he is usually depicted as being surrounded by animals and birds because he so loved them. But I once read something that goes a little more deeply into his true connection with them. It was said that he heard the voice of God in every creature's call; he saw the beauty of creation in every detail and design of the natural world; he felt the breath of God in every breeze that ruffled a bird's feathers or rustled the leaves of a tree. Thus, he sensed the presence of God in every single living thing and he dedicated his life to that simple recognition. I love this, but for me, I take it even a step further in that I accept guidance or affirmation through the messages delivered by either the call of an animal or the movement of the natural world. For example, when we are deep in thought perhaps pondering a course of action, a dilemma or some decision to be taken, and we suddenly hear an animal noise that startles us, I often find it is an affirmation of what was being thought at that precise moment. Another example is when deep in thought and walking in country lanes, if a bramble should tear at you or, worse, slap you in the face, it could be a sign to say that we are thinking along the wrong lines in our search for a solution to a problem. These things are known as 'listening to the whispers of the universe' or, as I like say 'listening to God's messages'.

To illustrate this from one of my own experiences,

many years ago I was walking part of the Saint's Way in Cornwall. I had a simple map with directions but while in the middle of nowhere, the path ran out and I was having real difficulty following the instructions as it did not seem to relate to the lie of the land before me. I had already retraced my steps once, when I realised I was off route but did not know which field or which style I should be crossing next.

I took the plunge and crossed one of the styles only to be confronted by a very large and rather menacing looking cow at quite close quarters. It mooed loudly at me and stepped towards me which was enough for me to beat a hasty retreat. I tried a different direction and found after a few minutes that I had indeed finally found the right path again. I was grateful to that cow in 'heading me off at the pass' so to speak. You might find this a tad far-fetched but when you experience it for yourselves, you might start to get the message here. It is well known that in the Druid tradition to name but one of the old ways, each animal or bird held its own symbolic meaning. An interesting parallel is that their depiction of the blackbird which leads one into the deeper mysteries symbolised by the cave, is also featured on the icon of Elijah who sits at the entrance to a cave where a blackbird perches, holding the sacrificial wafer in its beak. Yet another snippet to add to this piece is that in Egyptian hieroglyphics, the illustration of the hare with its ears erect has the meaning 'listen, I am going to tell you something' and appears before some historical event is being told.

I find it quite wonderful to be able to embrace all life

into one system of unity and non-separation, and to know that help is at hand in the most commonplace of ways if only we expand our awareness to it.

Chapter 6

Holy bones in holy places

Some years ago I was on holiday in Italy exploring the stunningly beautiful coast of Amalfi. I was visiting the magnificent cathedral, the Duomo, in Amalfi town itself and found it very impressive as it held much history of its holy relics and their reverence and spiritual power. The story went that St Andrew's bones, which were now held in the crypt, once every so many hundred years, oozed a certain black oily substance which was reputed to have miraculous healing properties.

I went down into the crypt along with many other tourists and admired the beautiful inlaid coloured marble floors and pillars. On the wall was a painting some 300 years old depicting this miraculous oozing from the holy bones and the overjoyed faces of the people as the sick and infirm were healed. The crypt itself was dimly lit with the only focus of light directed onto a fine white marble statue of St Andrew who held in his right hand two finely engraved silver fish. You may remember from the scriptures that he was the disciple who was called from his livelihood as a fisherman to instead follow The Christ, who had said to him and his companions "Come with me and I will make you fishers of men". I also like the fact that the symbol of the fish representing Christianity comes from the initials I.C.X.C. thus abbreviating the name Ie/sus/ Christ/os. These abbreviated letters also spelled out in Ancient Greek the name for fish, hence the symbolic connection. Beneath this statue of St Andrew was a casket containing some of his actual bones, the very bones that surround this mystical legend. I couldn't simply file past along with all the other visitors so I sat down in one of the pews and remained in a sort of silent meditative state. After a while, as the queues died down, the place became almost empty but still I remained, almost glued to the spot. A concierge who sat in dedicated vigilance in the crypt finally came over to me and in her broken English she said "You like it here!". I turned to her and was about to say something like "Oh yes, it's lovely", but as I opened my mouth, a choked sob came out and I became inexplicably tearful, but I managed to say "Yes" with a big smile. The emotion I felt was as if I myself had received this fabled miraculous healing and I was brimming with thanks, praise, gratitude, humility, relief, all rolled into one. It was a memorable experience and yet another example of how I have unknowingly managed to tap into certain energies abound in these special holy places.

Many of us love to visit old churches, chapels, cathedrals and monasteries without having any religious leanings. It is my belief that on some higher level, the soul always yearns to know more of its connection with God / the Source / the Universal Spirit / All That Is, call it what you will (but, please, not the Mind or the Ego), and by being drawn to holy places, it is like a magnet that brings us a little closer to our divine connection with our individual spirituality. So enjoy these wonderful places with their awe-inspiring structures of architectural brilliance, their breath-taking stained glass, their statues, sculptures, paintings, inlaid floors, decorated ceilings and their holy relics; they are there for each one of us to gain a glimpse of something so much greater than ourselves. It is no coincidence that the word 'inspire' comes from the Latin 'to breathe in'; thus, we breathe in a greater knowing of what we are and what we may elevate ourselves to become, should we choose to do so.

Chapter 7

The power of music

Much has been written about the power of music and how it can inspire and convey a wealth of feeling, thanks to the skill of the composer, the choice of instruments, the rhythm and structure of the piece and, of course, the virtuosity of the performers. What amazes me is that, in my opinion, some of the most extraordinary pieces of music ever written are for the glory of God (and I include all religions and beliefs here). If all of the world's music were ever fully catalogued, I am willing to bet that works in honour of the Divine would far outweigh in sheer volume any other type of music. To me this is proof enough of the importance of having something supremely spiritual in our lives in that we strive to express it in music.

I once read that when Handel was composing 'The Messiah', his butler had entered the room with a tray of food, only to find his master on his knees gazing upward in animation with tears streaming down his face. His butler rushed to his aid and when Handel was able to speak, he said that it was as if the entire heavenly host of angels were present and singing the Hallelujah Chorus which he was writing at the time. How blessed he was to have heard that. The Messiah in its entirety is surely a true masterpiece.

In our more ordinary lives, we can often receive something from music that we may be in need of at the time. I find it particularly interesting that when we hear a popular song in our head, there is often a message in the lyrics that we should take note of. This has happened for me many times over the years; sometimes just absent-mindedly hearing a snatch of a tune before even knowing which song it was.

Then, when paying attention to the lyrics, I found that it echoed the very sentiment of what I was feeling at the time; sometimes even delivering the solution to a problem or suggesting a line of action to take when I felt I was at a crossroads.

Here's a fascinating experience I had during a concert in Wells Cathedral last year. I was listening to a piece I had not heard before - The Organ Concerto by Poulenc and had closed my eyes and must have drifted into what is known as the 'alpha' state of mind (not quite fully conscious but definitely not asleep). I became aware of a card in front of my eyes with writing on it. The card was a vivid midnight blue with silver writing on it and the words read "*.....just passing through......*"

After a while I opened my eyes and the music came flooding back in but I remembered clearly what I had seen. I am unsure of whether this was referring to my own life journey or whether it was some other discarnate being wishing to convey the brevity of our lives, but it was a profound experience and felt strongly significant in some way.

Chapter 8

Spiritual nourishment

It was a Christmas Day when these thoughts came to me; of what it means to some to have the Christ Spirit in our lives. Two months earlier, I was in Bethlehem visiting the Church of the Nativity, and something our Palestinian guide, a devout Christian, said about the significance of the Christ Child being born in a stable and laid in a manger had a powerful impact on me. As we have now come to understand, the manger was not the stable itself, but a hewn-out trough into which the animal fodder would have been placed. Shaped rather like an old stone sink, it was a suitable receptacle to place a baby in when there was "no crib for a bed". The symbolism of this is quite beautiful; that the Christ Child was being shown as the 'food, ie. nourishment' for mankind. Such a simple representation but one that had eluded me thus far.

During the same trip to the Holy Land, part of our rich and varied itinerary was to visit the chapel at Tabgha by the Sea of Galilee. This chapel had been built to commemorate the miracle of the feeding of the five thousand with five loaves and two fishes for the crowds who had gathered to hear the Sermon on the Mount. The old mosaic floor beneath the altar table bore a beautiful illustration of two fish on either side of a basket of bread which, curiously, only showed four loaves within it. I then learned that the artist had not 'made a mistake'. The fifth loaf was the actual blessed bread brought to each service for the taking of Holy

Communion. I loved the symbolism of this in that it brings the story to life right here in the present day by completing the number of loaves from the ancient story to becoming the on-going reminder that we receive "our daily bread" of spiritual nourishment. The added meaning of this is also to make clear that we are always given what we need for each day, one day at a time. It made my day.

To echo this theme of spiritual nourishment, I want to tell the story of Saint Davit Gareja of Georgia, Eastern Europe. He was one of the Desert Fathers and came from Mesopotamia where he was outcast for his religious beliefs and was deported. Interesting that this land today is called Syria where much the same is still happening. He arrived with one of the Brothers of his faith called Lucian who was a devoted servant to Davit. Having both traveled in very arduous conditions, they were relieved to find some rain water which had collected in the crags of some rocks, so they partook of this water and sheltered there awhile. The story goes that two deer with their fawns drew close and to their astonishment, allowed Lucian, under Davit's direction, to take milk from her into a bowl. Davit offered up this bowl of milk to give thanks, for he saw it as a gift from God, and when he made the sign of the cross over it, the milk immediately turned into curds and the two starving monks were able to eat and be filled from it. The deer came to them every day (except Wednesdays and Fridays; interestingly the two days when Orthodox Christians traditionally fast) to allow them to take milk, so they were able to settle there and hollowed out caves in the rock for their shelter. Gradually, their reputation as holy men spread to the outlying villages and when a crippled child was cured by their word of prayer, other devotees began to join them and in time a hermitage was built nearby, but Davit and Lucian chose to remain in their austere cave dwellings, being utterly devout, pious men.

When Davit made his sacred pilgrimage to Jerusalem, he brought back a mere stone from the Holy City and this stone is still revered to this day in the chapel of the monastery as many believe it to have healing properties. I have had the good fortune of visiting this Monastery of Davit Gareja and have climbed the mountain leading up from the old hollowed out cave dwellings. At the summit you can see the bleak desert landscape stretching out eastward to the border with Azerbaijan.

In the caves near the summit are ancient frescoes dating back to the 6th century (Georgia was Christianised by St Nino in the 4th century) and were no doubt painted by those early hermitage monks who settled there to be near St Davit. On the icon depicting St Davit, is shown the tame deer at his feet, and in many ways he is seen as a forerunner of St Francis, a holy man truly in tune with the animal kingdom.

I would like to end this chapter with the following quotation: "Mankind is hungry, but the feast is there, though it is locked up and hidden away". My own simple interpretation of this is that if we truly seek spiritual truth and nourishment, then we must be prepared to do more than just scratch the surface. The immense and deeply complex nature of Christ cannot really be taken at face value; there is so much more to be discovered as you unwrap the mysteries veil by veil. It is a life's work but the rewards are rich indeed. True Christmas blessings on this holy day would be that each and every one of us may receive what we need in order to help our understanding of how the Christ Spirit can blossom within us.

Chapter 9

Glimpses of life after death

Back in the 1970s, I experienced two deaths within one week. The first was my own father whom, unfortunately, I did not know well, other than having vague memories of his drifting in and out of my early childhood until the legal separation of my parents when I was about eight. After that, I can only remember three very brief occasions when we met, albeit for only a few minutes. He was such a stranger to me that I did not even visit him in hospital just before he died because of my doubt about whether there was anything to be said that would make any difference at that late stage in our estranged relationship. I was aware that I might be tempted to speak to him of my regret that he'd been so irresponsible in his role of being my father. I certainly knew that I would not have been ready at that stage to forgive him for the misery he had caused our family.

I told my mother that if she chose to go to his funeral, I would accompany her, otherwise I wouldn't be going. My sister and brother had also opted out. Mother and I decided we would attend and we took our Spiritualist hymn books with us and quietly sang the 23rd Psalm while all around us were wailing in their black veils as the Greek Orthodox priest recited the prayers all on one note in a manner so unfamiliar to our ears. When we got back home, I suddenly felt so tired that I could not keep my eyes open, so I took an enforced nap and fell into a deep sleep. After about an hour I was back to normal again but did not really understand quite what had just happened. When I returned home to London I received the sad news that my dear friend Peter, a handsome actor, who had cancer had died at the age of only 29. To my astonishment **the date and time of his death was at exactly the same time as when I had been forced to rest after my father's funeral.** It was as if I was in some way needed to assist in Peter's passing over but, of course, I can offer no proof to substantiate this.

I felt sad that I had not seen him in the months prior but he had stopped all visits because he didn't want anyone to see him looking so ill and without his hair which he had lost due to chemotherapy. Within the year, I went to see a clairvoyant woman who did not know me nor had any information about me, and she accurately described my father as a younger dapper man with his black wavy hair and 'pencil' moustache; evidently the way he preferred to be remembered. She told me that I had walked and talked with him many times in the spirit world to discuss our estranged life and that through these ethereal meetings, I had forgiven him. I had previously been angry about his poor attempt at being a responsible father and how he had negatively affected all lives in our family through his compulsive gambling habit which I now, of course, know is an addictive illness. She explained that when he had been shown the trail of destruction he had left behind him after his death, he was truly shocked and remorseful. She also expressed his deep regret that 'his ship had never come in', that he'd never had the life he had hoped for.

Then she said "And who is Peter?" and began to run her fingers through her hair saying excitedly "Look at this! Look at this!" It was not until a few weeks later that I understood the meaning of this. I had bumped into one of Peter's closest friends, the only one allowed to visit during those final months. He told me that when Peter's condition became so utterly final, they had stopped the chemo treatments **and that his hair had grown back thicker than ever.** This seemed a remarkable piece of spiritual evidence from a clairvoyant without any knowledge of my friend or his circumstances, nor could she have picked this up from me as I did not know this about Peter's final condition. In the Spiritualist Churches, occurrences like this are what they hold dear as **proof of survival** after physical death.

It seems to me that over the years, this belief has gradually crept into the main stream of popular culture and I am glad to say that I had this knowledge and understanding from an early age. It has become a key component in the piecing together of what I understand our 'invisible' life to be about; that the body is a temporary vehicle inhabited by an indestructible and eternal soul and that on the demise of the body (which 'returns to dust'), it returns to the Divine Source or Universal Spirit or whatever name you wish to use.

Chapter 10

No such thing as coincidence

We have all, at one time or another had experiences where things have turned out in a way that we could not have imagined or anticipated. We hear the common phrases, "what are the chances of <u>that</u> happening" or "it was obviously meant to be", etc. We can choose to believe that life and all its events are just a series of random happenings or that these land-marks are somehow pre-ordained and are simply waiting for us to meet each one; rather like an ethereal string of pearls strung out into the future and we travel along the thread encountering each pearl in turn. People have argued that such a destiny cannot exist if mankind is meant to have free-will. Personally, I am oddly comfortable with the paradox that both can and do co-exist, just not necessarily in a format that we can easily consider or accept.

Many years ago, I read a wonderful biography of a well-known psychic medium called Estelle Roberts who did much of her work in the 1930s and 40s. This book made such an impression on me that I can still recall many of the true stories it contained. I would like to repeat here one of them that demonstrates the topic of 'coincidence' in quite an extraordinary way. It tells of a man who had lost his wife and was so immersed in the sorrow of his bereavement that he found life meaningless and no longer worth living. He therefore began to plan ending his own life. He was sitting on a park bench mulling over his devastating loss with the unbearable thought that his wife had simply ceased to exist and was gone forever when a gust of wind sprang up. A loose sheet of someone's discarded newspaper blew towards him and wrapped itself across his legs. As he picked up the news-sheet, his eye fell upon an advertisement for "An evening with Estelle Roberts, the famous medium" at the Royal Albert Hall.

He decided he would go along to see if she could give him any information about his dear wife having any sort of continued existence in this 'spirit world' of which he knew nothing. He sat through the entire evening listening to the medium's many accurate descriptions of the departed loved ones of members of the audience and the detailed messages offering evidence of their survival after physical death. When there was no personal message for him, with a heavy heart he made up his mind that he would indeed end his life that night. As Estelle Roberts received applause for her evening's work, she pointed to him, singling him out and said "....and you, sir, please come to see me afterwards". He was astonished but did as he was asked. Back stage, she immediately said to him with her hand outstretched "Give to me what you have in your pocket". He tried to deny her request but she was insistent and he finally handed over the bottle of poison with which he was going to kill himself. Estelle then explained that his wife was indeed alive in the spirit world and that it was she who had guided him to come to the meeting that night so that his life could be saved and his grief eased.

I think this is one of the most wonderful examples of

not only survival of the soul after death, but also a brilliant case of 'no such thing as coincidence'. So instead of dismissing similar events in your own life as just 'lucky', consider that you might have been guided to, hypothetically, be standing on that particular corner at that particular time to encounter an old friend with whom you had lost touch and who was just about to emigrate and be lost to you forever, giving you a chance to say your goodbyes.

Chapter 11

A story of Georgian saints

On All Saints' Day, my thoughts turn to what it takes to be or become a saint. There are many who do good works or those who sacrifice their personal lives to care for another or who seek to assist in the face of war-torn countries or natural disasters, and I take my hat off to all of them for their dedication and selflessness. But when I think of the saints of old who gave up their lives in the most torturous of ways, I am beyond admiration for their willingness to meet their death for the sake of their unshakeable faith in Christ/God. It somehow makes me feel ashamed that I would not be able to find such courage and conviction of my own beliefs. I remember having this thought when I heard the story of how 6000 monks were slaughtered by the Persian army in 1616 because they would not convert to Islam. They were all made to kneel at the altar of their mountain shrine above the monastery of St Davit Gareja in Georgia (eastern Europe) where they were, one by one, all beheaded. When I voiced my misgivings about my own lacking faith, I was reminded by our translator guide that these devout people had God in their daily lives so strongly and tangibly that there would have been 'no contest' about what to do. In fact, the story goes that the elders had said that if any wished to save themselves, they gave their blessing for them to do so, and two of the monks chose to hide.

But when these two saw the ethereal golden crowns

that God bestowed upon the souls of the monks who gave up their lives, they came out of hiding and offered themselves to also be killed.

As I stood in that very same chapel, with its 6th century frescos where this ghastly event took place, I became almost hysterical with grief. It was as if I had taken on the lamentation of their suffering and their sacrifice. It affected me so deeply that I could not stop crying for three days. This experience led me to becoming baptised in the Holy Spring of St Nino, the girl saint who Christianised Georgia in the 4th century.

So let us not dismiss the saints, let us honour them and be in awe of how they carried out their lives according to their own true convictions of what they believed in. Let us at least follow our own true conviction of what we believe in and never deny another just to save face or to avoid being stigmatised or be ashamed of our true motives.

Chapter 12

Spiritual healing

Much has been written and debated about the ability to heal through the laying on of hands. Healing circles and groups have existed for approximately a century, particularly within the Spiritualist Churches and, I am glad to say, even in some of our 'ordinary' churches, though I suspect not all denominations. It is now common knowledge through the sciences that an electro-magnetic field surrounds all living things, including, of course, we humans. Kirlian photography even produces an image of this energy emanating from, for example, the tips of our fingers. It is also well-observed that some healers appear to have a stronger more effective ability than others to bring about a change for the better in a client, but it eludes logic when we try to establish the reasons for this. It seems to be accepted that some simply 'have the gift' and some do not. I would like to suggest that we all potentially have the ability to heal but that there is a certain 'whittling down' of criteria before a final good result might be achieved.

First of all, there needs to be an element within the person that actually wishes to be able to help another; that has the compassion and sympathy when seeing suffering in another. Then there follows a willingness to learn a little more about it in order to adhere to good practice including what today's appropriate and acceptable boundaries are. The next stage is to be brave enough to face the fear of 'failure', i.e. that their healing may appear to have made no difference, thus producing the subsequent temptation of giving up. I believe that healing takes place on so many different levels and that it is not for us to know what has made a difference or not, but to simply trust that in the higher scheme of things, something has made a difference. Next in the elimination process of a healer's efficacy is the cultivation of their **intention**, to truly desire to bring about some easing of symptoms, discomfort or pain for the sufferer. Finally, and very importantly, the healer must place their ego to one side and not seek pride, fame or glory by being able to say "I healed that person" or "it was thanks to **me**".

In regard to the receiving of payment in return for the service of healing, my opinion is divided. It is not the healer him or herself who has brought about the healing, but that they act only as a channel or conduit for this 'supernatural', even divine energy which is available to everyone. However, if that individual has discovered they have a remarkable gift and they choose to devote all of their usual working life hours to it, then, we all know that bills still have to be paid. Therefore, each healer must make this decision for themselves and their conscience. There is, however, something to be said for the fact that people tend to value something more if they have actually paid for it. A system often operated is one of donation with perhaps a percentage being given to charity. As for the 'right qualifications', it is my firm belief that there is no 'rubber-stamping' a good healer. You can do all the workshops and training courses you like, take all the exams, receive and frame your certificates, boast of your status as "Master of .... " etc, but it comes down to the fact that nothing will make you any better than another because it is a natural (some would say God-given) gift that you can either choose to use for the good of humanity or ignore it for whatever reason.

Without going into the details of the actual preparation and process of doing any healing, I feel I should include in this chapter the perhaps obvious point that the healer should, first and foremost, be well and stable in oneself, then to place all personal agenda to one side and to clear the mind of fleeting thoughts and distractions. It is a clear focus of intention that is required and this is a crucial ingredient of the process. Why not try it for yourself? You could lay your own hands upon yourself, your child or partner; even an animal. You might be surprised by the results but in any event, do not be discouraged. In the words of the Master Jesus, "You will do all these things and more. Go and do thou like-wise."

Chapter 13

A visit from Einstein

While watching television recently, I was suddenly aware of a dazzling bright light a short distance to the left of the screen, behind which was the plain wall of my sitting room. The light was a silvery electric blue and was shaped like a short bar rather than an orb (which I have often seen). I considered a trick of the light or a reflection from an image on the screen but try as I might, I could not replicate it. Within minutes, the news came on and the first item concerned the new scientific discovery of 'gravitational waves' out there in the universe; thus proving what Albert Einstein had always postulated, and they showed a picture of this famous genius. It made me smile as, for some unknown reason, I have always had a fondness for this man. Then I remembered why!

The story I am about to tell takes me back to 1976. A book I was reading at that time was a biography about Uri Geller (who, let me say, did a darn sight more than just bend spoons) and how he had claimed contact with extra-terrestrials. These beings had imparted to him statements about the nature of the universe which, at the time, were truly revelatory. They added that there had only ever been one human who had got close to the true nature of it, and that was Albert Einstein. I took this book with me to Paris for a holiday staying in a friend's flat.

One day, after miles of foot-slogging around the

beautiful sights of this city, I had come back to the flat for a rest before going out again in the evening. I must have dozed off for the next thing I knew, I saw in the distance surrounded in a blank grey mist, an old man walking towards me with a rather shuffling gait. He wore an old pale grey suit which was very creased and misshapen from never having been pressed and the jacket was done up by just one button in the middle, creating well-established creases across the midriff. He shambled right up to where I was lying and he leaned over me peering into my face. When I awoke with a start, I had a clear recollection of his features but did not know who he was. Weeks later, back at home, I was visiting a book shop during my lunch hour break from work. I had found a very amusing book of photos of important people doing silly things with cartooned captions which were hilarious. My mind could not have been further away from any serious thoughts of the universe as I sat there on the floor chuckling away. Suddenly, it was as if unseen hands had taken hold of my head and turned it to look sideways and slightly upwards to a different shelf of books. There, staring me in the face was a full cover picture of that very same face who had peered at me in Paris while I was resting. The book was a biography of Albert Einstein! I immediately bought the book and avidly began to read but try as I might, my brain just could not grasp the meaning nor explanation of the theory of relativity (and I take my hat off to those who can); however, I enjoyed reading about his life and marvelled at his intelligence and dedication. In the central pages was a collection of some old black and white photographs and one of them made my jaw drop. There was a photo of him looking **exactly** as I had seen him - the same pale grey baggy suit done up with one button in the middle, the same creases and general unkempt look with his wild, wispy, grey hair and that enigmatic smile. I was quite stunned. It was as if he had come to visit me those few weeks earlier in Paris to ponder "who is this slip of a girl interested in the universe and things beyond her realm of comprehension?".

In the last few years, science programmes have become ever more popular and I love the topics of time, space, the universe and all things futuristic, even though I still struggle to fully understand their concepts. If, in some parallel universe, I was someone who did understand all this stuff and had a brilliant mind instead of the rather sluggish one I currently have, perhaps Einstein would have utilised my abilities to thus impart further knowledge from his own brilliant mind to another in order to continue his work. I am only sorry I was not the right material he might have been looking for, but the fondness between us, I believe, still remains. And who knows - maybe some of today's geniuses are being inspired from the great minds that have gone before, whether they know the source of their inspiration or not. I am minded of the words from a piece of music called 'The Creation' by Haydn. **"The heavens are telling the glory of God, the wonder of His work displays the firmament".** I believe it is people like Einstein who had a real grasp of this "wonder of His work". I know that my own grasp is a spiritual one and to me it is worth more than any academic or intellectual knowledge and is certainly as valuable. The only downside is that this inner knowledge stays with me and me alone and cannot be shared for the good of humanity nor the advancement of knowledge. This has to be the job of the geniuses out there, the 'Einsteins' of this world; while I, in my own small world, quietly understand but cannot explain.

Chapter 14

Archie the chimney sweep and Jimi Hendrix

After I'd moved to London in 1970, I continued to visit my mother up in the Midlands at the weekend, and on the Saturday evening we would always go to her Spiritualist Church. We witnessed many things there over the years and there were many startling examples of clairvoyance, mediumship in its many forms, including, on one special occasion, transfiguration which has to be seen to be believed.

One of the members of the circle was a woman who regularly channelled a young boy called Archie, a chimney sweep from Victorian days when they used to send small boys up the chimneys to clean them. This little chap had apparently been killed by falling bricks. I was sitting in the circle between the woman and my mother when I noticed she began to fidget like a child who was not used to sitting still on a chair and her feet didn't seem to reach the floor. Archie's presence was recognised by the circle who greeted him, then he turned to me (the woman's eyes were closed) and with a cheeky grin he said in the broadest Cockney accent, "You're with that lady, ain't yer, Missus" indicating my mother the other side of me. "Yes, she's my Mum" I said. "Oh, and where d'yer live, then?" he said, but before I could answer, my mother chipped in and said "You find her, Archie!"

Back home in London a few days later, I was busying about my bedsit while listening to music by The

Incredible String Band. On the wall was a large psychedelic poster of Jimi Hendrix, another of my favourites at the time. Suddenly, one of my framed pictures fell off the wall! I examined it to see if the string had broken or the nail had loosened, but everything was still intact. It was all a bit strange. On my next visit to the church, Archie came through again to report that he had found me. My mother said laughingly, "Yes, and you knocked a picture down, didn't you!" He squirmed in his seat with embarrassment and said "Aw, I didn't mean to, Missus, I was just trying to straighten it", (It's true that it always hung slightly crooked.) He then proceeded to describe my room, saying that there was a box with a red light on it (my old hi-fi) and "snake-charming music coming out of it". (Imagine a boy from the Victorian era trying to describe 'hippy underground' music!) He added, "And there was this geezer with whiskers!" describing the poster of Hendrix with his curly mop and facial hair. It was an amusing episode at the church, but on a much more serious note, I want to tell you what happened the very first time my mother visited that church years earlier.

The medium, who also happened to be the minister of the church, was leading the session of clairvoyance when he began to clutch his neck as if in pain. "I have someone here who died of a broken neck" he declared. No-one spoke up from the large audience to 'claim' this 'visitor'. He spoke again, grimacing in pain, "Someone here must know this person who died of a broken neck. Please speak up, whoever this person belongs to." Still no-one spoke; and just to explain; the symptoms will persist for the medium as the 'calling card' until the departed soul has been identified. Then the symptoms subside as the medium makes the connection with the living person they 'belong to'. He repeated a third time "Will someone please claim this person who died of a broken neck". Still silence, until my mother finally spoke up with "I know of someone who died from an injury to the neck?". With much relief the medium said "Yes, you dear, thank goodness, at last!". He then described a scenario of armoured vehicles leaving a battlefield in haste with soldiers running after them, jumping onto the back to get away from the surprise attack in progress. He described in detail how this person had been attacked from behind 'commando style'; how his head had been jerked back and his throat being stabbed, **breaking his neck in the action!** This was a revelation to my mother as she had always grieved that the soldier had suffered a slow agony as he bled to death, but in fact, his death was instantaneous! The medium went on to explain that the soldier had waited all these years for some way of letting her know that his death was not the dreadful one she had always imagined. This soldier was her 18 year old brother, an Austrian in Hitler's army who were fighting in Zagreb trying to control the guerrillas in the old Yugoslavia. The year was 1944. I want to make it clear that no-one knew my mother prior to this event, nor had any inkling that she was Austrian. She was just a stranger who had turned up for the meeting. It was an extraordinary introduction to the workings of the Spiritualist Movement and she became an ardent member for the rest of her life. Together we learned many things and developed our psychic gifts which have played a part in both our lives.

Coming back to Jimi Hendrix, my mother was inexplicably fascinated by him whenever she saw him on TV. She didn't 'understand' the music but said "There's something special about him", but couldn't say what. She had somehow made a psychic connection with him because a few days before he died, she 'saw' an image of a covered stretcher being carried out of a basement flat of a large white house with black railings. When she saw it on the news, it was exactly as she had seen it days earlier. Several days later, while doing housework with nothing further from her mind than psychic matters, she saw him standing looking at her, way off in the distance. Then within seconds he drew near becoming life-sized standing facing her in her kitchen! She saw him as clear as day as a real living person and he had a quizzical look on his face and looked troubled. With her spiritual knowledge and compassion, I know she would have given him love and blessings to help him adjust to his 'new life'. Then he was gone and she wanted to run down the street and tell everyone about it, but who would have believed her. Several weeks later, he appeared to her again and this time he was smiling as if to say "Everything's OK now".

I cannot explain why such an enigmatic and talented musician would have made a connection with a humble, non-musical middle-aged woman like my mother, except to say that the agenda of souls bears little resemblance to that of living persons. When we talk of 'like attracts like', it is to do with the spiritual aspects of beings, not their occupation or social standing. Somehow, her particular energy and compassion was just what he needed to make sense of what had happened to him and she would have given it freely without the need of recognition or acknowledgement; something we could all learn from.

Chapter 15

Archangel Michael

For many years the name of Archangel Michael has turned up in my life; either through study, lectures, reading or discussion. It would appear that he is the Archangel who has been 'put in charge' of earthly matters and it is no wonder to me that he is almost always depicted as overpowering evil beneath his feet; whether that evil is represented as a devil-like figure, serpent or dragon-like creature. My favourite statue of him is the one that crowns the pinnacle of the cathedral spire atop Mont Saint Michel in northern France. He stands with a sword in his right hand raised high above his head and in his left hand he holds a circular object with which he suppresses the rise of the creature beneath his feet. The whole statue is covered in gold and when it glints in the sunlight it can be seen from a long way off. It is a powerful emblem of protection.

I have come to learn that, far from being some remote ethereal figure from ancient times that featured in the scriptures, he is a real and present being for us all and continues to be of service to mankind. One has only to call upon him for his assistance and he is present. I heard tell of someone who, while out walking in a town, had her wallet stolen from out of her hand by someone who ran swiftly past her. Having her wits about her, she immediately cried out **"Michael!!"**, whereupon the thief stumbled and dropped the wallet, then ran away. She gratefully retrieved it, but also gratefully gave thanks to Archangel Michael.

My own story also concerns attempted theft of money. I was standing at an ATM outside a supermarket. I had inserted my card and was about to begin a transaction when a woman behind me called out asking about where to get a trolley. I'd answered briefly and by pointing, but she persisted, and in a moment of extreme ill-judgment on my part, **I left the ATM** to step a few yards back to show her the trolley park. As I turned back, in the blink of an eye, a young boy sped in front of me, leapt to the machine, then ran away. The card was no longer halfway lodged in the slot and I realised to my horror he had stolen it. In a shocked state I ran inside the store and began to blurt out that the police should be called, when a young woman came in holding my card saying that **it was sticking out of the machine**! I thanked her profusely and made my apologies to the Customer Desk manager for my outburst.

As I recovered from the shock of what had happened, I tried to piece together what had <u>actually</u> happened. Either the older woman who distracted me was genuine and the young lad was an opportunist just waiting for an incident such as this, or they were working together as a team. Either way, the miracle for me was that at the precise moment that he ran to the ATM to seize my card, the machine instantaneously decided to 'swallow' it and he ran away empty-handed! Then, when the machine decided to make it 'reappear', the next customer just happened to be a totally honest young woman who immediately brought my card into the store. Lucky me! But the more I re-ran the scenario in my mind, I began to doubt whether the boy was even '**real**'. Those few seconds of panic seemed almost dream-like and surreal and I began to wonder if this experience was a warning from Spirit to never allow myself to be distracted like that ever again. And for that little lesson, if that is what it was, I thank Archangel Michael. If it **was** real, then the timings of the disappearance and reappearance of my card was truly miraculous, and again, I thank Archangel Michael for presiding over this occurrence and orchestrating a brilliant result for me.

So the next time you witness something negative occurring, whether it is a violent public altercation or you find yourself in immediate danger, perhaps as a victim of some crime, call upon Michael and I firmly believe that somehow, the situation will be diffused or resolved. Try it you have nothing to lose!

Chapter 16

Exorcism

Back in the mid 1980s I had the privilege of belonging to a closed psychic circle which I attended weekly for 5 years. It was an important commitment to doing some extraordinary work of which much could be written. In addition to this, there was also a weekly 'open house' for the free giving of healing by a team of dedicated healers who welcomed all-comers. During this time, I knew a young woman from Ethiopia and she confided in me telling me of her own personal repeated nightmare of being killed and seeing the spirit of someone else leave her body. It was a terrifying experience for her and although she outwardly appeared happy, deep inside she was continually tormented and she showed signs of being a very damaged person. She also told me of two events that had taken place in her childhood that, without doubt, had contributed to her traumatisation. She had twice been captured as a small child by a marauding tribe who wore frightening masks while performing the rite of genital mutilation and on the second occasion, her epiglottis was removed! I cannot imagine how terrifying that must have been to a small child, and add to that the pitiful fact that she never told her parents, even though her mother knew something must have happened. On hearing her story, I recognised that some form of demonic possession was present and I invited her to come to the Healing Group for help. I should add here that I knew the leaders of the group as powerful healers with much experience of these matters and I gave them advance warning that I would be bringing this young lady so that they could prepare for some serious work to take place.

As we drove to the appointed place, my friend became more and more agitated saying she didn't want to go and that we should turn back, a classic sign that whatever was possessing her knew that its time was up and was about to be removed from the 'hosting' body vehicle of my friend. By turning her away and filling her with fear, they could remain in situ to continue their ghastly influence on her. But they had me to deal with and I pulled out all the stops in consoling her and convincing her that we must go ahead. As we walked in, the circle was ready for us and knew exactly what to do as, no doubt, they had all been primed beforehand. They formed a firmly bonded circle around my friend who was seated on a chair in the centre. I was placed outside the circle as I was, at the time, too emotionally susceptible to take part but I became a sort of sentinel overseeing the proceedings. I was trapped on one side of the circle which filled the room and could not get to the door to stop other visitors from entering, so I kept a transfixed stare to form an invisible barrier at the entrance to protect from any interruption.

My friend looked absolutely terrified and kept looking at me with pleading and tearful eyes but I motioned to her to remain seated. The leading healer stood behind her with his hands on her shoulders and as he spoke, his voice rose in volume as he addressed the unwelcome possessing entity. I cannot say how long this went on for as it was like being frozen in time but the importance of the bonded 'battery-forming' circle surrounding them was imperative to being able to contain the exorcised entity to send it where it needed to go, rather than allowing it to enter into the very next vulnerable and susceptible person who could then become its new host.

After what must have been about 20 minutes and at the end of the session, my friend was smiling and looked very relieved. The moment the circle broke holding hands and returned to their seats, there arrived some elderly ladies who were regular visitors who would have been aghast to witness what had just taken place. I saw this as a miracle in itself, that the capsule of time was truly held 'frozen'. I took my friend back home to where her partner eagerly awaited her and he was overjoyed to see her looking so happy.

But there is a most interesting footnote to this story. When I next attended our closed circle, I was told that at the point of the demonic entity's departure, it had tried to enter the healer himself to make him strangle her! He had to fight with all his strength to keep his hands firmly on her shoulders and not close in around her neck! A truly extraordinary experience all round but I thank God that I was the catalyst to help this young woman by leading her to the right source of help.

My closing words concern whether the results of any similar event would be permanent or not and my understanding of it is this: that it all depends on whether we allow any chink in the armour of our spiritual protection. It is these such chinks that are seized upon by demonic entities whose sole purpose is to wreak havoc, perhaps in order to re-live their lives of depravity and destructive elements of behaviour. So my final advice is this: never allow negative or destructive thoughts to dwell and grow within you; never allow fear to overtake your knowledge of who you are and what you can achieve through good use of your own choices; never perpetuate negativity by repeated immersion in the darker aspects of jealousy, envy, revenge, anger and aggression; and most of all, never vacate possession of your own soul through the repeated and addictive use of mind-altering substances such as drugs and alcohol and, in particular, hallucinogenics, otherwise you tread a very dangerous path that none can navigate safely.

Chapter 17

A narrow escape

On a spiritual workshop I attended many years ago, I recall the following quotation given: "The will of God will never lead you where the grace of God cannot sustain you". I thought about this for a long time and pondered to myself the question "But what about suicides?". Surely these poor souls were handed out more than they could bear? I now wonder that perhaps the people who end their own lives are missing any belief or understanding of how the grace of God works; that they were not aware of what clues were being given to help them or how they could rise above their lot in life, instead of believing there was nothing left for them. I do not pass any judgement here, just a pondering that in their sorrow, perhaps they missed little opportunities to take a different viewpoint, to receive help, and to count their blessings instead of their 'curses'.

Here is an anecdote from my own past experience of how I believe I was sustained by the grace of God, though I admit that I didn't have any concept of this at the time. It was back in the 1970s and I had been invited by a friend to have coffee and listen to his latest music acquisition; some rock album or other. I had one leg in soft plaster from a minor accident a few days earlier, so I was seated comfortably in an armchair with the plastered leg up on a stool. He handed me a pair of high-fidelity headphones which I put on to get the full impact of the music. But after less than a minute, for some inexplicable reason, I quite suddenly removed the headphones. Within seconds, I began to hear a strange, high-pitched creaking noise and, as if on automatic pilot, I put my arms up over my head and threw myself over the side of the armchair as the entire ceiling came crashing down in huge, thick chunks of solid plaster! One of these huge chunks struck me on the side of my body, cracking my ribs, as I hurled myself out of its path.

Had I remained seated with the headphones on, I would not have heard the ominous warning of the creaking sound and would have been struck directly on the top of my head; and I think it could have killed me. What was it that made me remove the headphones when I was really enjoying what I was listening to? I cannot call it intuition because I was unaware consciously of any danger. Was it instinct? Again, I sensed no impending danger. I believe it was a case of 'the grace of God' working in my favour using angelic intervention to save me from either death, brain damage or, at the very least, serious head injury. At the time, I thought it was just a lucky escape, but looking back now, I believe something much more precious happened, and it saved my life.

On a similar and lighter theme, I once saw a joke cartoon of a man trapped on the roof of his house in rising flood waters. A man in a rowing boat came by and called out to him to jump aboard but he replied "No, it's alright, God will save me". As the waters rose, another boat drew near, but again he sent them off saying "No, it's alright, God will save me". As he clung to the chimney on the roof of his house, a rescue helicopter hovered above but again, he turned them away with "No, no, God will save me". The poor man drowned and when he got to the 'Pearly Gates' he asked God why He did not save him. God sternly replied "Good Heavens, man, I sent two boats and a helicopter! What more do you want?".

So, for me, the moral of these two tales is to keep on the lookout for how the grace of God can work in your own life to provide comfort and sustenance in times of stress, even in a life-saving situation.

Chapter 18

Living in a haunted house

Back in the late 1960s after I had left home, I found myself living in a flat within a huge rambling Victorian mansion set in large grounds complete with stables and a long driveway from the road. The flat which I shared with a work colleague was, I later learned, in what would have been the servants' quarters at the top of the house, and in the three years I was there, I witnessed many inexplicable occurrences which I would like to relate.

One rainy day, I had returned home and placed my big black umbrella into a bucket and stood it in the corner of the kitchen, its curved bamboo handle leaning into the right angle of the walls. After making supper, I was doing some ironing and would place clothes on a hanger on a line stretched across one side of the kitchen. Something made me look up and I watched in astonishment as the umbrella handle began to rock from side to side while still standing in the bucket. It had not been touched, knocked or dislodged in any way. I could do nothing but continue with my ironing and again my eye was drawn to look up. My black dress which had been hanging motionless on the line was now rocking back and forth as if someone had deliberately knocked it to start it moving.

In the winter time, I used to light the little gas fire in the bedroom to take the chill off the air (forget central heating, it hadn't been invented!) and I had run out of matches, so I went into the kitchen to light a spill (a narrow wooden taper) from the pilot light of the primitive water heater. I cupped my hand around the flame and walked the short distance back into the bedroom, but on entering it, the flame immediately went out yet there was no draught. I retreated to the kitchen for second lighted taper and this time was much more careful in shielding the flame. But as soon as I entered the bedroom, again the flame just extinguished itself before my own eyes. I was too spooked to try a third time. I got into bed with blankets and quilt tucked tightly around my head for warmth and was tired and ready for sleep when I had one of the most startling experiences of my life. Someone had sat on the end of my bed! I could feel the weight and pressure near my feet, and my heart nearly jumped into my mouth. I was petrified with shock and could only think of holding my breath and pretending to be asleep. However, within seconds, I was covered in what I can only describe as a golden wave of warmth and light as if I was being comforted and soothed rather than being made to feel afraid. The next thing I knew, I was waking up the following morning and the memory of what had happened came flooding back in. I simply could not imagine how I could have possibly fallen asleep after such a fright.

Another equally startling experience happened one mild Sunday afternoon. My flatmate had gone away for the weekend and I was alone, writing in the sitting room. After a couple of hours, I decided it was time for a break and went into the kitchen to make coffee. As I re-entered the sitting room, imagine my horror to find that the gas tap at the side of the little fire had been turned on and I could hear the gas hissing out! I quickly turned it off, then spun round looking behind furniture to see who had played such a horrible trick, but of course there was no-one there. Anyone in the rest of the house would have had to come up two flights of stairs to reach my attic flat and I would have heard them on the stairs.

I used to love watching live music and often would come home late into the night. The house owner's daughter Mary used to light a big log fire in the entrance hall of the house which was a huge space with large stained glass windows either side of a stone fireplace. There was a wide, long staircase leading to the upper floor and a long balcony stretching across the width of the house which then turned at right angles to a further balcony, thus encasing the whole space with its polished balustrades. One winter's evening after a late rock concert, I lingered by the welcoming fire to warm myself, just sitting there quietly in the dark. As I finally began to mount the stairs, I became aware that someone was watching me from the opposite balcony with a very stern, disapproving and angry stare. I did not dare look across to where this person was standing but kept my head down and hurried up the further two flights of stairs to my flat.

Then there were the several occasions when my brand new black leather boots were being tampered with. They had a decorative buckle and strap at the side and I kept finding the strap tucked back in under the buckle so that when I released it again, the strap would stick out, rather annoyingly, at an angle. I checked with my flatmate and any other possibilities but couldn't get to the bottom of it. I finally suspected Mary's little daughter who might have been wandering around the house while I was out but this too was denied. One Christmas Eve, everyone in the house (it was all bedsits and flats) had gone away for the holiday, even Mary's husband and two children had gone on in advance to their family home in the country. As there was only the two of us left in the entire house, Mary invited me down for a festive drink, but before I went downstairs to her ground floor flat, I checked to look at my boots in the kitchen and they were as they should be. However, when I returned upstairs, lo and behold, the strap was again turned back under the buckle! It was as if I was given final proof that it had not been done by any living hand.

My mother who was a very psychic woman came to visit to help me piece together the remnants of the events I had been witnessing. The umbrella, dress and boots were all black in colour, as worn by the serving staff of older times; I was living in the servants' quarters; the angry one watching me as I returned home late was the fearsome housekeeper who gave the maid an utterly miserable time and the gas was how the poor girl ended her life. Of course, we had no proof to substantiate any of this, but when things happen that you cannot deny, I had no personal need to prove anything. We simply accepted that this poor soul was not at rest and she had been trying to alert my attention to her plight. I realised at a much later date that all she needed was my prayers for her to be at peace and to coax her beyond her dismal earthly experience of that life and move on to better things.

Should anything similar happen to you, I urge you to simply light a candle and offer your prayers or good wishes to whomever is present, for them to find acceptance of their situation, to find forgiveness of all concerned in their drama and to trust that they will find a final resting place of peace. I believe that they may then be able to become aware of their guardian angel or whomever has been appointed to the task of leading them to the light.

Chapter 19

Rescuing lost souls

Within the Spiritualist movement that I grew up with, as an adult, there were lesser known 'inner' groups or 'closed' circles set up for the purpose of 'Rescue Work' and over the years, I had the privilege of belonging to three such groups. What is involved in this work requires some explanation before I recount some of the more extraordinary examples of what I experienced and witnessed.

It is postulated that when a person loses their life in a sudden, unexpected or traumatic death, such as a fatal accident, suicide, murder, or where there is some serious unfinished business, whether of an ethical, judicial or emotional nature, the soul of that departed person does not always immediately make the transition to their new home of light. It is, as it were, between worlds; stuck in a particular light vibration that has no home in either place. It remains close to the earth vibration but cannot return to the gross matter of physicality; equally, it cannot transcend to the higher vibration of light (call it heaven, the spirit world or a higher dimension, if you will) because that soul either does not know that the body it inhabited has 'died' (I have heard of a departed husband who wondered why a place had not been set for him at the table!) or refuses to leave without acquiring whatever recompense it believes it deserves. So this troubled soul resides in a 'hinterland' of unrest and may remain there for a very long time until 'rescued' from either 'above' or 'below'.

Being rescued from 'above' would require some loving soul with angelic qualities to reach down and convince the poor being to let go and come with them to a better existence. But because of the level of vibration mentioned earlier, they would probably be unable to perceive this higher helper who equally would perhaps be unable to lower their own vibration sufficiently to communicate with the trapped soul. It seems that the only way such a soul can move on is to touch base with the vibration of gross matter from whence it came and then make the leap to a higher plane. It therefore falls to the Rescue Groups to assist in this essential process, but I must emphasise that this work should not be taken lightly. There are many deaths involving foul play and dark circumstances that require only the experienced to deal with such a situation.

One such example happened sometime after I had been invited to join two other women, whom I shall call A and B, in this work. They had been quietly sitting together while I was out of town, but I received a message that I should urgently visit them as soon as I returned later that day. When I got there they explained to me that B had taken on the soul of a poor woman trapped in a dark place and needed rescuing but that A was unable to assist because she had taken on the soul of the man who had brought about the demise of the trapped soul and would not let her go. The situation needed a third person (i.e. me) to intervene with the power struggle going on.

The story unfolded that this man had been having a rather one-sided affair with the woman who it seemed was very much under his domination. When he refused to release her from her sexual 'duties', she threatened to tell his employers (I had the sense of his being the keeper of an estate and that she was also in their employ). He had become so angered by her threat that he had bound her with rope and had thrown her into the river where she had drowned. When I tried to persuade her through B that she was no longer tied to this man, she cried that she was still petrified of him and she could see him menacingly coming towards her. I reassured her that she was safe now and that he could not harm her but she remained utterly glued to the spot and unable to move towards the light that I described for her. Meanwhile A continued to snarl and curse at us both and I had to come up with something quickly that would save the situation. I began to describe to B a cylindrical wall, like an open-topped chimney that I was building around her for her protection so that she could not see this vengeful, threatening man. I suggested confidently that her limbs were now free from the ropes and that she could look up and see the circle of shining light up above her. Slowly she gained confidence and began to rise upwards as I continued to talk encouragingly to her until finally she had made it and was gone.

However, the rescue did not end there. A continued to snarl aggressively saying "She was mine, she belonged to me!" Fortunately, B was now free to assist (as her tormented soul had now gone) and she gently reproached the man saying "No-one can own another person". What surprised us next was that the man broke down in tears saying how he had never had anyone to love him or care for him and this was why he had commandeered the woman to fulfil his needs. We were then able to gently convince him that if he were to now go up to the light himself, he would find his lost family who would welcome him home. A 'returned to herself' and we all marvelled at this 'double rescue' and the enormity of what we had achieved.

Another fascinating example was of a 'mass rescue' where several souls were all stuck together and unable to move on. After our opening prayers, I began to psychically see an old-fashioned tin soldier and I wondered if we might be dealing with a child. But then, as I watched, there was a diagonal peeling away of the tin encasement of the toy soldier (just like the old sardine cans that used to be opened diagonally with a key to reveal what was inside) and slowly from the bottom up, a full size soldier was gradually being revealed. First I could see the white tabbed socks and gaiters, then the kilt and the tartan drape of a Scottish piper in full regalia. As the picture revealed more and reaching up to his head, I saw to my horror that he had no face! It had been shot away and was a mess of blood. It was a shocking sight and turned my stomach over. This brave soul was the piper who had led the army into battle and he was right in the firing line. As we said our prayers for his release, A and B both described a stampede of the whole battalion all rushing forward in their need to also be rescued towards the light that was provided through the piper's release. It was as if the piper had held to his duty of leading the soldiers right to the very end and then leading them on to their higher life. It was a very moving experience.

Over the years I have been part of the rescue of dozens if not hundreds of examples of this rescue work but there is just one more example to be told here. A chap I knew used to work as a security guard and was called to patrol an area that had been fenced off at the foot of Avon Gorge after a young man had jumped to his death. During the evening, the guard heard the agonised voice of a young man saying "Oh no, what have I done!" and he answered him back asking what was the matter, even though he was alone and could see no-one else present. The young man said "I thought this would end it all but now I can see that nothing has changed. Oh, what have I done. What have I done!" The guard, being a down to earth sort of fellow said to him "Well you can't hang around here, mate. You'd best be off". Whether that did the trick or not, we'll never know, but I would like to think that because it was said with honesty and sincerity, that poor young man, realising the truth of his situation, would hopefully accept responsibility for his actions and move onwards and upwards without getting stuck between worlds.

So if ever you sense an unseen presence, instead of feeling fear, feel compassion and send them a little prayer that they move on to higher and better things. If you can call in a guardian angel, so much the better but please be warned not to take on any situation without sufficient knowledge of what you are dealing with and seek the help and support of more experienced workers in this field if you sense you are out of your depth. Just remember the necessary vibration required is love, compassion and forgiveness.

However, too much sympathy, naivety or gullibility could enable a lost or negative soul to latch on to you and could cause havoc in your own personal life. Be warned.

Chapter 20

Brought to the feet of God

Half a lifetime ago, I had the most amazing and important spiritual experience of my entire life. I must have been in my early thirties and, interestingly, I recently learned that spiritual experiences often occur around the age of 33, (perhaps because that was the age of Jesus when he returned to the Godhead). It is extremely important that I emphasise that this experience I am about to relate was absolutely no dream. It was either what is known as a 'lucid' dream or an experience in the 'alpha state', that deeply relaxed state of mind that happens just prior to falling asleep, but it was definitely an out-of-the-body experience.

The first sensation I had was that of being surrounded by white light as if enveloped in pure white clouds but their having no discernible shape. I sensed that I was mid-air and that I was travelling at great speed. It was as if I was outside an aeroplane caught in its slip-stream. I was wearing a vivid purple-violet coloured scarf around my neck and it was fluttering so vigorously in this slip-stream that it was whipping against my face. I became aware that the great speed I was travelling was not horizontal but, in fact, vertical! I was, quite literally, ascending straight upwards at a breath-taking speed. The sensation was quite bewildering and it was happening so rapidly and involuntarily that all I could do was go with it and allow it to happen. There was no way I could have put up any resistance. I then became aware that I was actually travelling towards something at a great distance above me but I did not know what. I tried to look up at the object of my destination but had to shield my eyes from the sheer brilliance of the light streaming down which was a dazzling white/gold. My hands were shielding my eyes but by peering through the cracks of my fingers I began to make out a gigantic figure standing looking down at me with arms outstretched in a posture of welcoming me. This being was enveloped in a brilliant white garment of huge folds down to the feet. The face was impossible to look upon; it was like trying to look at the sun, and the dimensions of this figure were measureless. As I got closer and closer it was as if I no longer existed as a separate being and that I simply merged as one with this majestic being. At the same time, I experienced a heavenly feeling of pure ecstatic bliss and this somehow correlated to a physical sensation of the most heightened orgasmic quality. This electrifying feeling was so overwhelming that I snapped back into my physical consciousness but continued to experience the orgasmic sensation while also having the feeling that I was rapidly falling back to earth and back into my body. It was the most awesome spiritual experience I have ever had and it has never to date been repeated.

I want to make it clear that at that time, I had no religious practice nor had any concept of what I now believe happened; that I was delivered to the feet of God/The Divine, so that I could have an inkling of the ultimate nature of what I am (and indeed what we all are), a spiritual being and part of the 'Kingdom of God', or, to use a secular term, the greater Whole or

Universal Spirit. Over the ensuing thirty plus years since this happened, I have read or heard about many spiritual references that describe some of the aspects of what I personally experienced. They are referred to as 'Going home to God'; 'merging with the One True Spirit'; 'The Unapproachable Light'; 'The Bride meeting the Bridegroom'; 'The Vesture of Light', and so on, and this has made me realise that what I experienced was exactly what these scriptural texts were referring to and describing, but they were all unknown to me at the time.

I have always felt it a great privilege to have been granted such an awesome experience of being in the presence of God or The Christ Spirit and it is one I can never forget or ever deny. Quite why I was singled out to receive this magnificent gift is something I cannot know the answer to, but I am deeply honoured and ever grateful. I have also considered that I was allowed that experience at a time in my life when I was deeply unhappy and needed a reason to believe life was worth living. I will end with some of the words from the Sermon on the Mount -"Blessed are the poor in spirit, for they shall see God". I am indeed blessed for without doubt, I was 'poor in spirit' at that time in my life.

Parting Words

It is my hope that you, the reader, have found something amongst these chapters that strikes a chord of recognition or perhaps has stirred a memory from your own experiences that you might have put down to mere 'coincidence'.

If I have shown a different perspective or an alternative viewpoint, then I have achieved my aim.

May you have many wonderful experiences of your own and remember what was quoted in the Introduction, "Ask, and it shall be given unto you" and allow the myriad of angelic messengers to become the interface between the two worlds of the ethereal and the physical in your own life.

About The Author

Throughout her life, Stella was often told by friends "You should write a book!" because she was always recounting little personal anecdotes which people often found interesting and enjoyable.

It wasn't until 2015 that she was finally convinced that she really should put pen to paper. In fact, this forceful encouragement came from a 'new' guardian angel who had been waiting in the wings (no pun intended) telling her in no uncertain terms to get on with it. The writing began as a blog, part of which has now become this first collection of anecdotes.

Stella lives in Somerset and continues to write about her many recollections of her own personal experiences and her understanding of our fascinating 'inner' life.